Alter? When the hills do.
Falter? When the sun
Question if his glory
Be the perfect one.

Surfeit? When the daffodil
Doth of the dew:
Even as herself, O friend!
I will of you!

The Mystery of Beauty
Poems by Emily Dickinson

Frank J. Miller

With tender majesty . . .

The Mystery of Beauty

Poems by
Emily Dickinson

By the Editors of Country Beautiful

COUNTRY BEAUTIFUL
Waukesha, Wisconsin

This is my letter to the world
That never wrote to me,—
The simple news that Nature told,
With tender majesty.

Heart, we will forget him!
You and I, to-night!
You may forget the warmth he gave,
I will forget the light.

COUNTRY BEAUTIFUL: *Publisher and Editorial Director:* Michael P. Dineen; *Vice President, Editorial:* Robert L. Polley; *Vice President, Operations:* Donna Griesemer; *Managing Editor:* John M. Nuhn; *Associate Editor:* Kay Kundinger; *Senior Editors:* Kenneth L. Schmitz, James H. Robb, Stewart L. Udall; *Art Director:* Buford Nixon; *Assistant Editor:* Wendy Weirauch; *Art Assistant:* Ann Baer; *Marketing Director:* Jeanie Holzwart; *Director of Sales:* Mary Moran; *Administration:* Roy Adolph; *Staff:* Rita Brock, Gay Ciesinski.

Country Beautiful Corporation is a wholly owned subsidiary of Flick Reedy Corporation: President: Frank Flick.

Library of Congress Cataloging in Publication Data

Dickinson, Emily, 1830-1886.
    The mystery of beauty.

    I. Country beautiful. II. Title.
PS1541.M9 1975   811'.4   75-42318
ISBN 0-87294-080-2

Joe Kirkish

CONTENTS

Introduction 6

The Altered Look of Seasons 8

Out of the Morning,
    Into the Night 30

Secrets of Creatures 40

Experiment of Green 60

The Mountain 90

By the Sea 96

The Designated Light 104

Introduction

In the almost 1,800 brief poems she wrote during her lifetime, Emily Dickinson pierces to the heart of the great universal mysteries of life, love, death and nature. She reveals the singular beauty to be found at the core of these themes in a terse, aphoristic, sometimes awkward style which, to a certain degree, reflects the uncompromising nature of her Puritan sensibility. It also manifests the sheer poetic power generated by the tension in her verse between the concrete New England world in which she lived and the cosmic concern of her Puritan soul.

The Dickinson family was by inheritance the quintessence of Puritan New England. Her father, Edward Dickinson, was educated at Yale, followed law as his profession, served in the state legislature and Congress, and was treasurer for almost forty years of Amherst College in Amherst, Massachusetts, the small town where the family lived, including Emily's mother, sister Vinnie and her adored brother Austin. Her father was demanding, possessive and remote, if not severe. Yet Emily observed, "If Father is asleep on the lounge, the house is full."

After receiving her education at nearby Mount Holyoke Female Seminary and Amherst Institute, Emily retired from the community, seldom leaving the family house, rarely coming down from her room, almost always dressed in white. The few men in her life, the subject of much conjecture, apparently were married and sometimes much older. Nonetheless she was passionate. She wrote to one of them, "The air is soft as

Italy, but when it touches me, I spurn it with a sigh, because it is not you." But the flames of her passion burned on words alone. Increasingly, she became precious of her person and her thought.

During the years between Emily's twentieth and twenty-fifth years, 1850 to 1855, American literature came to flower. Nathaniel Hawthorne's *The Scarlet Letter* and *The House of the Seven Gables,* Herman Melville's *Moby Dick,* the first edition of Edgar Allan Poe's collected poems, Henry David Thoreau's *Walden,* and Walt Whitman's *Leaves of Grass* all were published. But of these writers and others of the nineteenth century, only Melville, with his intense, Calvinistic concern for the eternal, interior conflict between Good and Evil, shares some common ground with her. Emily rejected the specific tenets of Calvinism, but her moral tone, angular and direct simplicity, spring from the Calvinistic tradition. Some critics have mistaken this simplicity for naiveté.

It wasn't until about 1858, when she was twenty-eight, that Emily began to write mature poems with any regularity. The years 1859 through 1865 were her most productive ones. Only three were published during her lifetime. But she soon accepted the fact that fame in her lifetime was not to be hers, which she expressed in a verse in 1863:

Fame of Myself, to justify,
All other Plaudit be
Superfluous—An Incense
Beyond Necessity . . .

After Emily's death in 1886, her sister found about nine hundred of her poems and she undertook to have them published. In 1890 a volume of 115 poems was published. Although Emily wrote most of her poems in one or more drafts before transcribing the final version, her first editors could not accept them as anything other than sketches for poems. The poems in the first books published of her work were thus "improved" and polished to conform with the conventions of punctuation and meter in poetry of the time. It wasn't until well into the twentieth century that her talent, vision and achievement were appreciated for their true worth.

The four lines quoted above are not those of a frustrated, discontented person. It is a mistake to think of Emily Dickinson's life as tragic or unfulfilled. It is not necessary to find a real flesh-and-blood lover for her. Poetry was her obsession. Her seclusion seems to have been a deliberate and conscious choice. In the Puritan and Transcendentalist tradition, she mastered life by removing herself from it. She removed herself to a distance from life, not to reject it, but to better understand it and herself. She mastered life by mastering her art. For it was through her poetic gift that she was able to come to terms with her private anguish and to resolve, at least partially, the tension between the concrete world and her Calvinistic soul. In the process she came to understand nature, which she revered; love, which was her ideal; and even to understand death, the subject of several of her poems. Hers was not a starved life as many have inferred; it was surely one of the deepest and richest ever lived.

Emily Dickinson can truly be called America's greatest poet of intelligence and ideas, but she does not *reason* at all. She does *see* with a vision born of a fierce fusion of mind and sensibility that is unique in our literature. She loves nature's objects for the spiritual truth they reveal, and her vision renders the universal abstractions into something palpable because she perceives behind them the truth that is the incandescent reality which burns in the heart of each of us. With this incandescence, she illuminates the mystery of beauty in the subjects she writes about. Significantly, light, as subject and symbol, is the focal point of several of her poems.

The uniqueness of her vision, its ability to fuse the concrete and spiritual, and, finally, to come to terms with, in this instance, death, are splendidly revealed in the following poem, one of the finest in our language:

Because I could not stop for Death,
He kindly stopped for me;
The carriage held but just ourselves,
And Immortality.

We slowly drove, He knew no haste,
And I had put away
My labor and my leisure too,
For His civility.

We passed the school, where children strove
At recess, in the ring.
We passed the fields of gazing grain,
We passed the Setting Sun.

Or rather, He passed us;
The dews drew quivering and chill,
For only gossamer my gown,
My tippet only tulle.

We paused before a House that seemed
A swelling of the ground;
The roof was scarcely visible,
The cornice in the ground.

Since then 'tis centuries, and yet
Feels shorter than the day
I first surmised the horses' heads
Were toward Eternity.

Robert L. Polley

Section I
The Altered Look of Seasons

Thomas H. Algire

*And nobody knows
that any brook is there . . .*

Have you got a brook in your little heart,
Where bashful flowers blow,
And blushing birds go down to drink,
And shadows tremble so?

And nobody knows, so still it flows,
That any brook is there;
And yet your little draught of life
Is daily drunken there.

Then look out for the little brook in March,
When the rivers overflow,
And the snows come hurrying from the hills,
And the bridges often go.

And later, in August it may be,
When the meadows parching lie,
Beware, lest this little brook of life
Some burning noon go dry!

APRIL

An altered look about the hills;
A Tyrian light the village fills;
A wider sunrise in the dawn;
A deeper twilight on the lawn;
A print of a vermillion foot;
A purple finger on the slope;
A flippant fly upon the pane;
A spider at his trade again;
An added strut in chanticleer;
A flower expected everywhere;
An axe shrill singing in the woods;
Fern-odors on untravelled roads,—
All this, and more I cannot tell,
A furtive look you know as well,
And Nicodemus' mystery
Receives its annual reply.

*An altered look
about the hills . . .*

David Sumner

Thomas H. Algire

A light exists in spring
  Not present on the year
At any other period.
  When March is scarcely here

A color stands abroad
  On solitary hills
That science cannot overtake,
  But human nature *feels*.

It waits upon the lawn;
  It shows the furthest tree
Upon the furthest slope we know;
  It almost speaks to me.

Then, as horizons step,
  Or noons report away,
Without the formula of sound,
  It passes, and we stay:

A quality of loss
  Affecting our content
As trade had suddenly encroached
  Upon a sacrament.

A light exists in spring
not present at any other period . . .

13

A something in a summer's noon,
an azure depth, a wordless tune . . .

PSALM OF THE DAY

A something in a summer's day,
As slow her flambeaux burn away,
Which solemnizes me.

A something in a summer's noon,—
An azure depth, a wordless tune,
Transcending ecstasy.

And still within a summer's night
A something so transporting bright,
I clap my hands to see;

Then veil my too inspecting face,
Lest such a subtle, shimmering grace
Flutter too far for me.

The wizard-fingers never rest,
The purple brook within the breast
Still chafes its narrow bed;

Still rears the East her amber flag,
Guides still the sun along the crag
His caravan of red,

Like flowers that heard the tale of dews,
But never deemed the dripping prize
Awaited their low brows;

Or bees, that thought the summer's name
Some rumor of delirium
No summer could for them;

Or Arctic creature, dimly stirred
By tropic hint,—some travelled bird
Imported to the wood;

Or wind's bright signal to the ear,
Making that homely and severe,
Contented, known, before

The heaven unexpected came,
To lives that thought their worshipping
A too presumptuous psalm.

Kent and Donna Dannen

SUMMER'S ARMIES

Some rainbow coming from the fair!
Some vision of the world Cashmere
I confidently see!
Or else a peacock's purple train,
Feather by feather, on the plain
Fritters itself away!

The dreamy butterflies bestir,
Lethargic pools resume the whir
Of last year's sundered tune.
From some old fortress on the sun
Baronial bees march, one by one,
In murmuring platoon!

Revisiting the bog!

The robins stand as thick to-day
As flakes of snow stood yesterday,
On fence and roof and twig.
The orchis binds her feather on
For her old lover, Don the Sun,
Revisiting the bog!

Without commander, countless, still,
The regiment of wood and hill
In bright detachment stand.
Behold! Whose multitudes are these?
The children of whose turbaned seas,
Or what Circassian land?

Ed Cooper

As imperceptibly as grief
the summer lapsed away . . .

Gerald Irish

As imperceptibly as grief
The summer lapsed away,—
Too imperceptible, at last,
To seem like perfidy.

A quietness distilled,
As twilight long begun,
Or Nature, spending with herself
Sequestered afternoon.

The dusk drew earlier in,
The morning foreign shone,—
A courteous, yet harrowing grace,
As guest who would be gone.

And thus, without a wing,
Or service of a keel,
Our summer made her light escape
Into the beautiful.

INDIAN SUMMER

These are the days when birds come back,
A very few, a bird or two,
To take a backward look.

These are the days when skies put on
The old, old sophistries of June,—
A blue and gold mistake.

Oh, fraud that cannot cheat the bee,
Almost thy plausibility
Induces my belief,

S. J. Krasemann

These are the days when skies put on
the old, old sophistries of June . . .

Till ranks of seeds their witness bear,
And softly through the altered air
Hurries a timid leaf!

Oh, sacrament of summer days,
Oh, last communion in the haze,
Permit a child to join,

Thy sacred emblems to partake,
Thy consecrated bread to break,
Taste thine immortal wine!

The maple wears
a gayer scarf . . .

AUTUMN

The morns are meeker
     than they were,
The nuts are getting brown;
The berry's cheek is plumper,
The rose is out of town.

The maple wears a gayer scarf,
The field a scarlet gown.
Lest I should be old-fashioned,
I'll put a trinket on.

The sky is low,
the clouds are mean . . .

BECLOUDED

The sky is low, the clouds are mean,
A travelling flake of snow
Across a barn or through a rut
Debates if it will go.

A narrow wind complains all day
How some one treated him;
Nature, like us, is sometimes caught
Without her diadem.

Thomas Peters Lake

THE SNOW

It sifts from leaden sieves,
It powders all the wood,
It fills with alabster wool
The wrinkles of the road.

It makes an even face
Of mountain and of plain,—
Unbroken forehead from the east
Unto the east again.

It reaches to the fence,
It wraps it, rail by rail,
Till it is lost in fleeces;
It flings a crystal veil

It reaches to the fence,
it wraps it, rail by rail . . .

On stump and stack and stem,—
The summer's empty room,
Acres of seams where harvests were,
Recordless, but for them.

It ruffles wrists of posts,
As ankles of a queen,—
Then stills its artisans like ghosts,
Denying they have been.

Robert Holland

There's a certain slant of light,
on winter afternoons . . .

There's a certain slant of light,
On winter afternoons,
That oppresses, like the weight
Of cathedral tunes.

Heavenly hurt it gives us;
We can find no scar,
But internal difference
Where the meanings are.

None may teach it anything,
'T is the seal, despair,—
An imperial affliction
Sent us of the air.

When it comes, the landscape listens,
Shadows hold their breath;
When it goes, 't is like the distance
On the look of death.

Malcolm Lockwood

Out of the Morning, Into the Night

Will there really be a morning?
Could I see it from the mountains?

OUT OF THE MORNING

Will there really be a morning?
Is there such a thing as day?
Could I see it from the mountains
If I were as tall as they?

Has it feet like water-lilies?
Has it feathers like a bird?
Is it brought from famous countries
Of which I have never heard?

Oh, some scholar! Oh, some sailor!
Oh, some wise man from the skies!
Please to tell a little pilgrim
Where the place called morning lies!

Lee Mann

A dew sufficed itself
and satisfied a leaf . . .

A dew sufficed itself
  And satisfied a leaf,
And felt,'how vast a destiny!
  How trivial is life!'

The sun went out to work,
  The day went out to play,
But not again that dew was seen
  By physiognomy.

Whether by day abducted,
  Or emptied by the sun
Into the sea, in passing,
  Eternally unknown.

G. Gene Johnson

S. J. Krasemann

Angels in the early morning
may be seen the dews among . . .

Angels in the early morning
May be seen the dews among,
Stooping, plucking, smiling, flying:
Do the buds to them belong?

Angels when the sun is hottest
May be seen the sands among,
Stooping, plucking, sighing, flying;
Parched the flowers they bear along.

Jack Bowers

The sun just touched
the morning . . .

THE SUN'S WOOING

The sun just touched the morning;
The morning, happy thing,
Supposed that he had come to dwell,
And life would be all spring.

She felt herself supremer,—
A raised, ethereal thing;
Henceforth for her what holiday!
Meanwhile, her wheeling king

Trailed slow along the orchards
His haughty, spangled hems,
Leaving a new necessity,—
The want of diadems!

The morning fluttered, staggered,
Felt feebly for her crown,—
Her unanointed forehead
Henceforth her only one.

Gary Ladd

Doom's electric moccasin . . .

THE STORM

There came a wind like a bugle;
It quivered through the grass,
And a green chill upon the heat
So ominous did pass
We barred the windows and the doors
As from an emerald ghost;
The doom's electric moccasin
That very instant passed.
On a strange mob of panting trees,
And fences fled away,
And rivers where the houses ran
The living looked that day.
The bell within the steeple wild
The flying tidings whirled.
How much can come
And much can go,
And yet abide the world!

39

Secrets of Creatures

THE SPIDER

A spider sewed at night
Without a light
Upon an arc of white.
If ruff it was of dame
Or shroud of gnome,
Himself, himself inform.
Of immortality
His strategy
Was physiognomy.

*A spider
sewed at night . . .*

S. J. Krasemann

Don Bleitz

A resonance of emerald . . .

THE HUMMING-BIRD

A route of evanescence
With a revolving wheel;
A resonance of emerald,
A rush of cochineal;
And every blossom on the bush
Adjusts its tumbled head,—
The mail from Tunis, probably,
An easy morning's ride.

THE BLUE JAY

No brigadier throughout the year
So civic as the jay.
A neighbor and a warrior too,
With shrill felicity

Pursuing winds that censure us
A February day,
The brother of the universe
Was never blown away.

The snow and he are intimate;
I've often seen them play
When heaven looked upon us all
With such severity,

Dan Sudia

A neighbor and a warrior too,
with shrill felicity . . .

I felt apology were due
To an insulted sky,
Whose pompous frown was nutriment
To their temerity.

The pillow of this daring head
Is pungent evergreens;
His larder—terse and militant—
Unknown, refreshing things;

His character a tonic,
His future a dispute;
Unfair an immortality
That leaves this neighbor out.

John Tveten

THE ROBIN

The robin
is the one . . .

The robin is the one
That interrupts the morn
With hurried, few, express reports
When March is scarcely on.

The robin is the one
That overflows the noon
With her cherubic quantity,
An April but begun.

The robin is the one
That speechless from her nest
Submits that home and certainty
And sanctity are best.

*A single term
of cautious melody . . .*

At half-past three a single bird
Unto a silent sky
Propounded but a single term
Of cautious melody.

At half-past four, experiment
Had subjugated test,
And lo! her silver principle
Supplanted all the rest.

At half-past seven, element
Nor implement was seen,
And place was where
    the presence was,
Circumference between.

John Tveten

Robert Carr

Before you thought of spring . . .

THE BLUEBIRD

Before you thought of spring,
Except as a surmise,
You see, God bless his suddenness,
A fellow in the skies
Of independent hues,
A little weather-worn,
Inspiriting habiliments
Of indigo and brown.

With specimens of song,
As if for you to choose,
Discretion in the interval,
With gay delays he goes
To some superior tree
Without a single leaf,
And shouts for joy to nobody
But his seraphic self!

The skies can't keep their secret!

SECRETS

The skies can't keep their secret!
They tell it to the hills—
The hills just tell the orchards—
And they the daffodils!

A bird, by chance, that goes that way
Soft overheard the whole.
If I should bribe the little bird,
Who knows but she would tell?

I think I won't, however,
It's finer not to know;
If summer were an axiom,
What sorcery had snow?

So keep your secret, Father!
I would not, if I could,
Know what the sapphire fellows do,
In your new-fashioned world!

HOPE

Hope is the thing with feathers
That perches in the soul,
And sings the tune without the words,
And never stops at all,

And sweetest in the gale is heard;
And sore must be the storm
That could abash the little bird
That kept so many warm.

I've heard it in the chillest land,
And on the strangest sea;
Yet, never, in extremity,
It asked a crumb of me.

*Hope is the thing
with feathers . . .*

Ed Cooper

Olive Glasgow

A toad can die of light!

A toad can die of light!
Death is the common right
  Of toads and men,—
Of earl and midge
The privilege.
  Why swagger then?
The gnat's supremacy
Is large as thine.

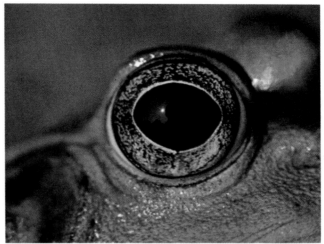

Paul E. Taylor

How public, like a frog . . .

I'm nobody! Who are you?
Are you nobody, too?
Then there's a pair of us—don't tell!
They'd banish us, you know.

How dreary to be somebody!
How public, like a frog
To tell your name the livelong day
To an admiring bog!

50

So hidden in her leaflets,
lest anybody find . . .

So bashful when I spied her,
So pretty, so ashamed!
So hidden in her leaflets,
Lest anybody find;

So breathless till I passed her,
So helpless when I turned
And bore her, struggling, blushing,
Her simple haunts beyond!

For whom I robbed the dingle,
For whom betrayed the dell,
Many will doubtless ask me,
But I shall never tell!

Leonard Balish

52

MOTHER NATURE

Nature, the gentlest mother,
Impatient of no child,
The feeblest or the waywardest,—
Her admonition mild

In forest and the hill
By traveller is heard,
Restraining rampant squirrel
Or too impetuous bird.

How fair her conversation,
A summer afternoon,—
Her household, her assembly;
And when the sun goes down

Her voice among the aisles
Incites the timid prayer
Of the minutest cricket,
The most unworthy flower.

When all the children sleep
She turns as long away
As will suffice to light her lamps;
Then, bending from the sky

With infinite affection
And infiniter care,
Her golden finger on her lip,
Wills silence everywhere.

S. J. Krasemann

Her parasol was seen
contracting . . .

Michael & Christine Fong

THE BUTTERFLY'S DAY

From cocoon forth a butterfly
As lady from her door
Emerged—a summer afternoon—
Repairing everywhere,

Without design, that I could trace,
Except to stray abroad
On miscellaneous enterprise
The clovers understood.

Her pretty parasol was seen
Contracting in a field
Where men made hay, then
      struggling hard
With an opposing cloud,

Where parties, phantom as herself,
To Nowhere seemed to go
In purposeless circumference,
As 't were a tropic show.

And notwithstanding bee that worked,
And flower that zealous blew.
This audience of idleness
Disdained them, from the sky,

Till sundown crept, a steady tide,
And men that made the hay,
And afternoon, and butterfly,
Extinguished in its sea.

57

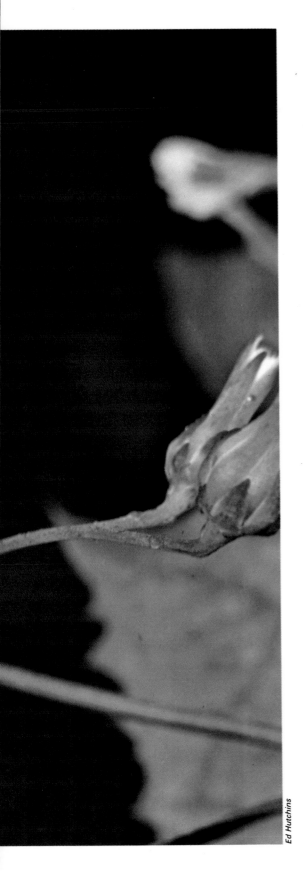

Ed Hutchins

To vanquish other blooms . . .

THE BEE

Like trains of cars on tracks of plush
I hear the level bee:
A jar across the flowers goes,
Their velvet masonry

Withstands until the sweet assault
Their chivalry consumes,
While he, victorious, tilts away
To vanquish other blooms.

His feet are shod with gauze;
His helmet is of gold;
His breast, a single onyx
With chrysoprase, inlaid.

His labor is a chant,
His idleness a tune;
Oh, for a bee's experience
Of clovers and of noon!

Experiment of Green

The mushroom is the elf of plants . . .

THE MUSHROOM

The mushroom is the elf of plants,
At evening it is not;
At morning in a truffled hut
It stops upon a spot

As if it tarried always;
And yet its whole career
Is shorter than a snake's delay,
And fleeter than a tare.

'Tis vegetation's juggler,
The germ of alibi;
Doth like a bubble antedate,
And like a bubble hie.

I feel as if the grass were pleased
To have it intermit;
The surreptitious scion
Of summer's circumspect.

Had nature any outcast face,
Could she a son contemn,
Had nature an Iscariot,
That mushroom,—it is him.

Ed Cooper

Joe Kirkish

*Still the
punctual snow . .*

New feet within my garden go,
New fingers stir the sod;
A troubadour upon the elm
Betrays the solitude.

New children play upon the green,
New weary sleep below;
And still the pensive spring returns,
And still the punctual snow!

New fingers stir the sod . . .

To make a prairie it takes a clover
And one bee,—
One clover, and a bee,
And revery.
The revery alone will do
If bees are few.

64

To make a prairie . . .

*I hide myself
within my flower . . .*

WITH A FLOWER

I hide myself within my flower,
That wearing on your breast,
You, unsuspecting, wear me too—
And angels know the rest.

I hide myself within my flower,
That, fading from your vase,
You, unsuspecting, feel for me
Almost a loneliness.

My flowers raise their pretty lips . . .

As children bid the guest good-night,
And then reluctant turn,
My flowers raise their pretty lips,
Then put their nightgowns on.

As children caper when they wake,
Merry that it is morn,
My flowers from a hundred cribs
Will peep, and prance again.

Lee Mann

The daisy follows soft the sun . . .

The daisy follows soft the sun,
And when his golden walk is done,
  Sits shyly at his feet.
He, waking, finds the flower near.
"Wherefore, marauder, art thou here?"
  "Because, sir, love is sweet!"

We are the flower, Thou the sun!
Forgive us, if as days decline,
  We nearer steal to Thee,—
Enamoured of the parting west,
The peace, the flight, the amethyst,
  Night's possibility!

The grass so little has to do,
I wish I were the hay!

THE GRASS

The grass has so little to do,—
A sphere of simple green,
With only butterflies to brood,
And bees to entertain,

And stir all day to pretty tunes
The breezes fetch along,
And hold the sunshine in its lap
And bow to everything;

And thread the dews all night, like pearls,
And make itself so fine,—
A duchess were too common
For such a noticing.

And even when it dies, to pass
In odors so divine,
As lowly spices gone to sleep,
Or amulets of pine.

And then to dwell in sovereign barns,
And dream the days away,—
The grass so little has to do,
I wish I were the hay!

William A. Bake

Experiment of green . . .

A little madness in the Spring
Is wholesome even for the King,
But God be with the Clown,
Who ponders this tremendous scene—
This whole experiment of green,
As if it were his own!

David Sumner

What right had fields
to arbitrate in matters ratified?

I worked for chaff, and earning wheat
   Was haughty and betrayed.
What right had fields to arbitrate
   In matters ratified?

I tasted wheat,—and hated chaff,
   And thanked the ample friend;
Wisdom is more becoming viewed
   At distance than at hand.

The leaves, like women, interchange
sagacious confidence . . .

GOSSIP

The leaves, like women,
   interchange
   Sagacious confidence;
Somewhat of nods,
   and somewhat of
   Portentous inference,

The parties in both cases
   Enjoining secrecy,—
Inviolable compact
   To notoriety.

S. J. Krasemann

*To invest existence
with a stately air . . .*

To venerate the simple days
Which lead the seasons by,
Needs but to remember
   That from you or me
They may take the trifle
   Termed mortality!

To invest existence with a stately air,
Needs but to remember
   That the acorn there
Is the egg of forests
   For the upper air!

In keen and quivering ratio . . .

For each ecstatic instant
We must an anguish pay
In keen and quivering ratio
To the ecstasy.

Jerome Drown

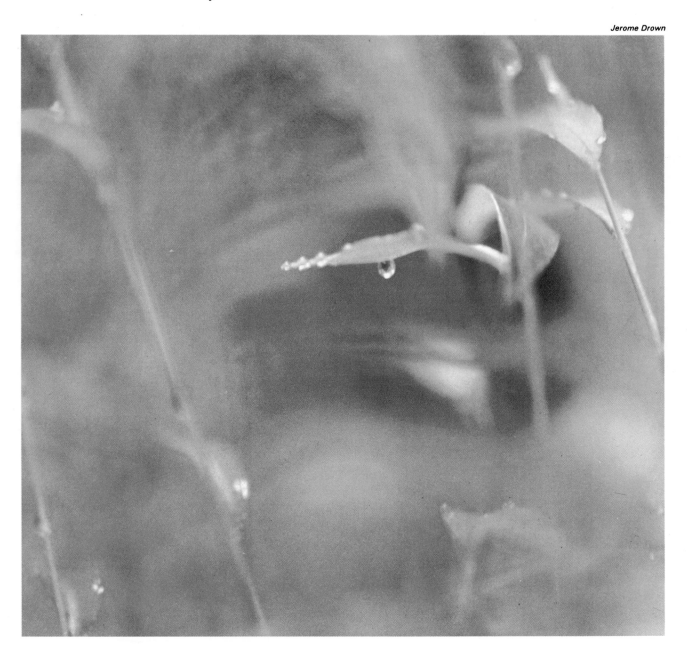

The pretty people in the woods
receive me cordially . . .

The bee is not afraid of me,
I know the butterfly;
The pretty people in the woods
Receive me cordially.

The brooks laugh louder when I come,
The breezes madder play.
Wherefore, mine eyes, thy silver mists?
Wherefore, O summer's day?

James Fain

THE WIND

Of all the sounds despatched abroad,
There's not a charge to me
Like that old measure in the boughs,
That phraseless melody

The wind does, working like a hand
Whose fingers brush the sky,
Then quiver down, with tufts of tune
Permitted gods and me.

When winds go round and round in bands,
And thrum upon the door,
And birds take places overhead,
To bear them orchestra,

I crave him grace, of summer boughs,
If such an outcast be,
He never heard that fleshless chant
Rise solemn in the tree,

As if some caravan of sound
On deserts, in the sky,
Had broken rank,
Then knit, and passed
In seamless company.

That old measure in the boughs,
that phraseless melody . . .

Shostal

We never know how high we are . . .

We never know how high we are
Till we are called to rise;
And then, if we are true to plan,
Our statures touch the skies.

Section V
The Mountain

The mountain sat upon the plain
in his eternal chair . . .

THE MOUNTAIN

The mountain sat upon the plain
In his eternal chair,
His observation omnifold,
His inquest everywhere.

The seasons prayed around his knees,
Like children round a sire:
Grandfather of the days is he,
Of dawn the ancestor.

National Park Service

90

David Dale Dickey

Inebriate of air am I . . .

Inebriate of air am I,
And debauchee of dew,
Reeling, through endless summer days,
From inns of molten blue.

Nature
rarer uses yellow . . .

Nature rarer uses yellow
  Than another hue;
Saves she all of that for sunsets,—
  Prodigal of blue,

Spending scarlet like a woman,
  Yellow she affords
Only scantly and selectly,
  Like a lover's words.

Ed Cooper

National Park Service

I'll tell you how the sun rose,
a ribbon at a time . . .

A DAY

I'll tell you how the sun rose,—
A ribbon at a time.
The steeples swam in amethyst,
The news like squirrels ran.

The hills untied their bonnets,
The bobolinks begun.
Then I said softly to myself,
"That must have been the sun!"

· · · · · · · · · · ·

But how he set, I know not.
There seemed a purple stile
Which little yellow boys and girls
Were climbing all the while

Till when they reached the other side,
A dominie in gray
Put gently up the evening bars,
And led the flock away.

You left me boundaries of pain
capacious as the sea . . .

BEQUEST

You left me, sweet, two legacies,—
A legacy of love
A Heavenly Father would content,
Had He the offer of;

You left me boundaries of pain
Capacious as the sea,
Between eternity and time,
Your consciousness and me.

THE OUTLET

My river runs to thee:
Blue sea, wilt welcome me?

My river waits reply.
Oh sea, look graciously!

I'll fetch thee brooks
From spotted nooks,—

Say, sea, take me!

Ed Cooper

100

THE SEA OF SUNSET

These are the banks
of the Yellow Sea . . .

This is the land the sunset washes,
These are the banks of the Yellow Sea;
Where it rose, or whither it rushes,
These are the western mystery!

Night after night her purple traffic
Strews the landing with opal bales;
Merchantmen poise upon horizons,
Dip, and vanish with fairy sails.

Norman Knabusch

But no man moved me till the tide
went past my simple shoe . . .

BY THE SEA

I started early, took my dog,
And visited the sea;
The mermaids in the basement
Came out to look at me,

And frigates in the upper floor
Extended hempen hands,
Presuming me to be a mouse
Aground, upon the sands.

But no man moved me till the tide
Went past my simple shoe,
And past my apron and my belt,
And past my bodice too,

And made as he would eat me up
As wholly as a dew
Upon a dandelion's sleeve—
And then I started too.

And he—he followed close behind;
I felt his silver heel
Upon my ankle,—then my shoes
Would overflow with pearl.

Until we met the solid town,
No man he seemed to know;
And bowing with a mighty look
At me, the sea withdrew.

Section VII
The Designated Light

That long shadow on the lawn . . .

Presentiment is that long shadow on the lawn
Indicative that suns go down;
The notice to the startled grass
That darkness is about to pass.

Max Tharpe

THE WHITE HEAT

Dare you see a soul at the white heat?
   Then crouch within the door.
Red is the fire's common tint;
   But when the vivid ore

Has sated flame's conditions,
   Its quivering substance plays
Without a color but the light
   Of unanointed blaze.

Least village boasts its blacksmith,
   Whose anvil's even din
Stands symbol for the finer forge
   That soundless tugs within,

Refining these impatient ores
   With hammer and with blaze,
Until the designated light
   Repudiate the forge.

Frank Aleksandrowicz

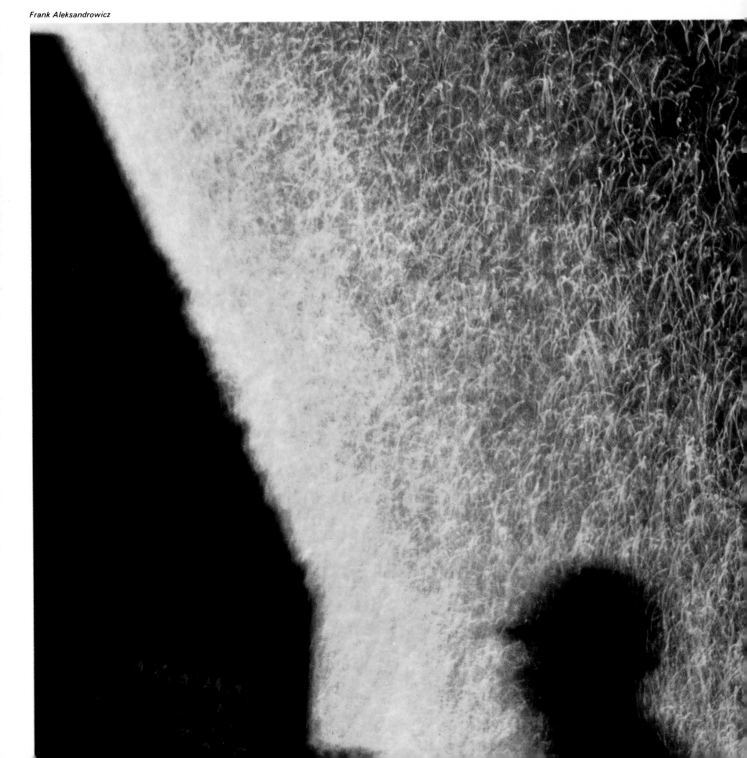

They perished in the seamless grass . . .

THE BATTLE-FIELD

They dropped like flakes, they dropped like stars,
  Like petals from a rose,
When suddenly across the June
  A wind with fingers goes.

They perished in the seamless grass,—
  No eye could find the place;
But God on his repealless list
  Can summon every face.

On her divine majority obtrude no more . . .

June B. Aschenbach

The soul selects her own society,
Then shuts the door;
On her divine majority
Obtrude no more.

Unmoved, she notes the chariot's pausing
At her low gate;
Unmoved, an emperor is kneeling
Upon her mat.

I've known her from an ample nation
Choose one;
Then close the valves of her attention
Like stone.

James Vosmek

Motionless as peace . . .

THE
FORGOTTEN
GRAVE

After a hundred years
Nobody knows the place,—
Agony, that enacted there,
Motionless as peace.

Weeds triumphant ranged,
Strangers strolled
    and spelled
At the lone orthography
Of the elder dead.

Winds of summer fields
Recollect the way,—
Instinct picking up the key
Dropped by memory.

111

The drop of anguish . . .
that scalds me now . . .

I shall know why, when time is over,
And I have ceased to wonder why;
Christ will explain each separate anguish
In the fair schoolroom of the sky.

He will tell me what Peter promised,
And I, for wonder at his woe,
I shall forget the drop of anguish
That scalds me now, that scalds me now.

Ron Sterling